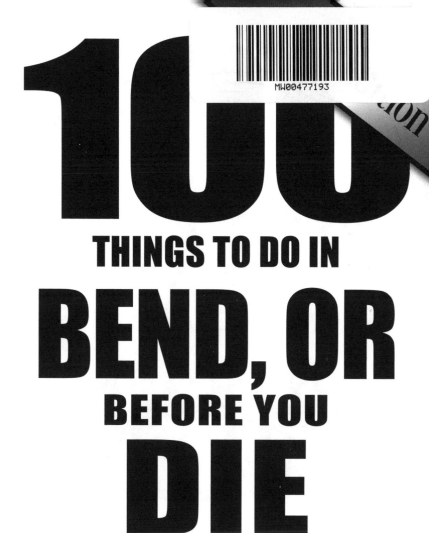

100

THINGS TO DO IN

BEND, OR

BEFORE YOU

DIE

100

2nd Edition

THINGS TO DO IN

BEND, OR

BEFORE YOU

DIE

• •

JOSHUA SAVAGE

REEDY PRESS

Library of Congress Control Number: 2022936981

ISBN: 9781681063782

Design by Jill Halpin

All photos are by the author unless otherwise noted.

Printed in the United States of America
22 23 24 25 26   5 4 3 2 1

DEDICATION

Once again, I dedicate this book to my wife and daughters. Through travel and exploration, we have become a stronger and tighter family. You all make this journey of life so much more rewarding and fun. I am forever grateful for these precious memories we make through our adventurous experiences.

CONTENTS

• •

Music and Entertainment

Sports and Recreation

● ●

● ●

Culture and History

Shopping and Fashion

• •

PREFACE

For many years Bend, Oregon, remained a small mill town on the Deschutes River, not easily accessible or known for its natural wonder. Fast forward to the present. The population of the area has swelled rapidly with no signs of slowing. The pandemic accelerated this trend, and it seems Bend is no longer a secret. Now, this once sleepy town is a mecca for outdoor enthusiasts, beer connoisseurs, foodies, and anyone else who appreciates spectacular landscapes, fun, and adventure. Honestly, Bend is about as epic as a place can get.

Yet, with growth comes responsibility. Most people here remain civil, friendly, and respect nature and each other. "Be nice. You're in Bend." is a local slogan that carries weight. Probably the time spent outdoors is what makes most everyone happy. For this reason, this book is heavier on outside activities than on anything else. When a place has mostly sunny days during the year and is surrounded by nature, how could it not? Let us intentionally work toward keeping it that way.

When I first visited Bend, I instantly fell in love. The moment I stepped out of the car, the smell of juniper trees and ponderosa pines filled the crisp, fresh morning air. Seeing the snowcapped Cascade Mountains in the backdrop, I suddenly felt like the weary traveler who had been searching for Shangri-La and found it. Although my family had no plans to stay permanently, here we are, proud residents of Bend. The more I explore, the more I love the area.

● ●

And although Bend is the most popular hub in the area, Central Oregon has much more to offer: Redmond, La Pine, Sunriver, Sisters, and the rest of Deschutes, Crook, and Jefferson counties, and even a bit beyond. The high desert of Oregon shares a climate and vibe that creates a unique destination worthy of any traveler's bucket list.

This second edition of *100 Things to Do in Bend Before You Die* features many new destinations and updated information. It has always been a daunting task to choose only 100 activities in a place where so many people want to live or at least visit.

Opinions and tastes differ, but I chose based on conversations with longtime locals, devoted tourists, and, naturally, my own experiences. Read thoughtfully and try to fully experience each activity, and remember, this book is only a small taste of what the high desert has to offer. Many other secrets await. By writing this book, my hope is that others will discover, enjoy, and respect one of the most wonderous places on Earth, Central Oregon.

Get in touch to share your opinions or suggest future destinations. And please, explore responsibly.

For regular updates on the endless list of things to do in Central Oregon, join our popular Facebook group @100+ThingsBend or find me on Instagram and Facebook @ultimatescavenger. Email: ultimatescavenger@yahoo.com

TAKE THE BEND PLEDGE

As mentioned in the preface, Bend is a special place. People here respect each other and their surroundings. In fact, @VisitBend has created a pledge that encourages all locals and visitors to equally share responsibility and help to ensure that Bend stays special for years to come. Please take the time to read the pledge.

1. Smile, say please & thank you, give right-of-way, and simply slow down.

2. Adventure and explore in a manner that is respectful to the land, wildlife, and the people you share it with.

3. Plan and prepare for your time on the trails, in the mountains and on the water.

4. Walk more, drive less, and stick to established trails, routes, and parking areas.

5. We must take care of the places that take care of us; we are all visitors here.

FOOD AND DRINK

BECOME A
BEER AFICIONADO
ON THE BEND ALE TRAIL

Stouts, IPAs, pilsners, sours, ales, oh my! The choices are endless. Beer is a way of life in Central Oregon. Ever visited a hop spa? Tried beer yoga? Participated in a beer relay race? Somehow, locals have managed to integrate the tasty beverage into almost everything imaginable. With over 20 breweries and counting, the region boasts some of the best brews in the entire country and takes the lead when it comes to creating new ways to enjoy beer. There seems to be a festival every other weekend to celebrate: Bend Brewfest, Oktoberfest, The Little Woody, High Gravity Fest, and many more. If you don't have a favorite type of beer, you might by the time you visit the many breweries or attend the festivals! A few favorites are sprinkled throughout the book.

TIP

Stop by Visit Bend to grab the newest, revamped version of the Bend Ale Trail passport or download the app. Make your way to each brewery in at least one section featured on the trail and get your passport stamped. Drinking a beer at each brewery is not required (designated drivers can claim a prize as well), but why miss out on the fun!? When you are done, return to Visit Bend and show your stamps to get a well-deserved prize (and bragging rights)! Distillers, cideries, and wineries are featured in the passport as well. Want to know anything else about Central Oregon? While at the visitor center, be sure to ask the knowledgeable crew. Visit Bend is the perfect starting point for any trip in the area.

Visit Bend
750 NW Lava Rd., Ste. 160, 541-382-8048
visitbend.com/bend-ale-trail

RELISH SOME GROWN-UP TIME
AT VELVET

Need some grown-up time away from the young ones? Find a sitter or leave the kids with the grandparents and spend an evening at Velvet. Grab a bite to eat downstairs, then go upstairs to a sort of speakeasy to try a drink or a few. The dimly lit setting, replete with comfortable couches, is the perfect place to kick back and relax over arguably the best cocktails in Bend. They have their own take on many libations, and even infuse yerba mate into several of their delectable concoctions. The Mojito la Argentina is second only to those made right in Cuba. The blueberries in the Blue Velvet are deliciously intoxicating. Since Velvet doesn't open until 5 p.m., expect them to stay open late, often providing a chilled vibe and some of the best nightlife in Bend.

805 NW Wall St., 541-728-0303
velvetbend.com

TRY EVERYTHING ON THE MENU
AT PLANKER SANDWICHES

Okay, it may be difficult to try everything on the menu at Planker Sandwiches, but most likely you will go back time and time again. Then, you may be tempted to get the same menu item as last time because it was so delicious, but deep down you really want to try something new. The best suggestion? Bring a group of people, have everyone order a different item, and share. More than a sandwich shop, Planker has paninis, burgers, salads, and soups. Even breakfast is available all day. Agreeable portions and fresh ingredients make the shop the go-to place for a consistently satisfying meal. My personal favorite is the Italian. Once you've eaten a Planker sandwich, Subway and Quiznos will never taste the same.

824 NW Wall St., 541-317-5717
plankersandwiches.com

EXPLORE A NEW WORLD OF FLAVOR
AT WILD ROSE

Whether you're eating at a local food truck or dining in the priciest restaurant, Bend has a fair share of diverse cuisine for a city our size. To stand out takes creativity and flavor. Wild Rose exceeds expectations. A local favorite, the restaurant specializes in northern Thai, a cuisine meant to be experienced with all five senses. Chef Paul Itti's delicious dishes consist of decades of his family's recipes and are meant to be shared so that your entire table gets a chance to enjoy the many flavors. Lunch, dinner, and takeout are available. If you've never tried Thai food, let this restaurant be your first adventure into the unknown. If you have, then expect your taste buds to be delightfully surprised. The family's newest restaurant, Sen Hot Pot, overlooks Mirror Pond and is also worth a delicious visit.

Wild Rose
150 NW Oregon Ave., 541-382-0441
wildrosethai.com

Sen Hot Pot
69 Newport Ave., Ste. 100, 541-385-6479
senhotpot.com

SATISFY YOUR SWEET TOOTH
AT CRAVIN'S

So much candy there is barely room to walk around inside of this children's heaven! Literally, kids can't pass by Cravin's Candy Emporium without lingering at the window and begging to go inside. It's hard for parents to say no, and why should they? Treat the kids (and yourself) to the many colors that jump out as you are surrounded by every candy imaginable. A library card catalog filled with different types of gum, PEZ dispensers of all the favorite characters, a wall full of sour candy, giant jelly beans, root beer barrels, gelato, gummies of all kinds, orange slices, cotton candy, popcorn, toys, games; I think you get the point. In the back of the store the original *Willy Wonka* movie continually plays on a large flatscreen. What's really cool is that many of the cast members (including Charlie and Willy Wonka) have actually visited a Cravin's location and their autographed pictures hang on the wall. Probably no other place in Oregon has so many different types of candy!

818 NW Wall St., 541-617-9866
cravinscandy.com

MAKE NEW FRIENDS
AT A FOOD TRUCK LOT

The food truck craze hit Central Oregon a long time ago and has yet to slow down. And why should it? Often, food truck lots breathe new life into areas. They become the local neighborhood hangout, an after-work spot to chill, or just an opportunity to spend time with friends or family. These modern-day entertainment hot spots have everything one could desire: drinks, fire pits, games, live music, and more. The food choices seem endless, and each lot has its own distinctive vibe. A growing number of trucks have popped up outside of Bend as well. In fact, Central Oregon has too many food trucks to name, but the following page has a list of the lots where most of them reside. Hopefully, I didn't leave any out, but they continue to open so quickly it's hard to keep up! Visit them all to make the wisest choice about a favorite.

The Patio at 9th Street Village
9thstvillage.com/food-carts-bend-oregon

General Duffy's Waterhole in Redmond
generalduffys.com

Midtown Yacht Club
midtownyachtclub.com

Spoken Moto
spokenmoto.com

On Tap Bend
ontapbend.com

River's Place
riversplacebend.com

The Lot
thelotbend.com

The Podski
thepodski.com

The Office at Silver Moon Brewing
silvermoonbrewing.com/the-office

The Bite Tumalo in Tumalo
thebitetumalo.com

The Barn in Sisters
thebarninsisters.com

Wild Ride Brewing in Redmond
wildridebrew.com/food

DO YOUR BEST JACK NICHOLSON IMPRESSION
AT WORTHY BREWING

A first visit to Worthy Brewing might make one curious as to why memorabilia featuring Jack Nicholson and the author Ken Kesey are strewn throughout the building. The reason? The Douglas fir bar tops, tabletops, and benches may look like ordinary wood, but it was sourced from the Oregon Mental Hospital, where the 1975 Oscar–winning *One Flew Over the Cuckoo's Nest* was filmed. If this alone isn't enough reason to visit, the brewery has no shortage of delicious food. The menu suggests excellent beer and food pairings that are carefully chosen by the chef. Try the pizza, made with fresh herbs straight from the brewery's own greenhouse. Worthy also leads the way in beer innovation. In fact, the owner, in conjunction with Oregon State University, created the now popular Strata hop used in many beers across the country. Worthy's Strata IPA beer is a Bend favorite (and mine)!

495 NE Bellevue Dr., 541-639-4776
worthybrewing.com

EXPERIENCE WHERE THE PAST MEETS THE PRESENT
AT THE BOX FACTORY

In which section should we add the Box Factory? It could fit into any category because this part of town has it all—food, entertainment, shopping, and history. Once a part of the Brooks Scanlon mill, box factories stored leftover scraps of lumber. This wood was used to make pencils, boxes, and other useful items. The mills closed in the 1980s, but rather than demolish the building, some creative and forward-thinking individuals decided to refurbish the original structure while maintaining its history. A major project indeed, and another amazing example of how Bend preserves and respects its past. Today, the Box Factory has over 35 local merchants with an amazingly diverse range of services. The list is too long to name them all, but this is a special part of town, one worth frequenting often.

550 Industrial Way
boxfactorybend.com

IMAGINE A TRIP TO ITALY
AT BONTA

Why bother with a trip to Italy when you can experience the world's best gelato right here in Bend? No joke, Bonta Natural Artisan Gelato makes some of the best handcrafted gelato I have ever tasted, and believe me, with two daughters who love ice cream, I have tried a lot. After a yearlong trip traveling the world, the owners, Jeff and Julie, wanted to capture the exotic flavors they encountered and bring them back to Bend. They then studied under two Italian gelato masters to hone their skills. Now, using ingredients from local businesses, they make everything from scratch and continually customize their own unique recipes. Flavors like Tumalo Lavender and Honey, Oregon Strawberry Rhubarb, and Thump Coffee can't be found anywhere else. My personal favorite is the Dulce de Leche with Sea Salt, but try as many flavors as you like and hear the stories behind them before deciding your favorite. When you taste the gelato here, you will never be satisfied with store-bought ice cream again.

920 NW Bond St., #108, 541-306-6606
bontagelato.com

SIP A BREW
WITH A SWEET VIEW
AT BEND BREWING COMPANY

Of all the breweries in town, Bend Brewing Company boasts perhaps the most enviable location. The second oldest brewery in Bend has one of the sweetest views of the Deschutes River where it meets Mirror Pond. Super family friendly, you can dine, drink, or play cornhole in the large courtyard overlooking the water or keep warm near the heated outdoor fire pits during the cold weather. In fact, BBC has deep roots in the community and makes ample use of the courtyard year-round with fundraisers, events like Yoga on the Pond and Rhythm and Brews, and other fun activities you may not associate with typical breweries. Sports fans will also be delighted to catch their favorite game on the big screens inside. The owners and staff have seriously thought of something for everyone to enjoy, an all-in-one place to hang out and have fun. Their newest taproom, Waypoint, recently opened at The Grove in Northwest Crossing as well, another excellent spot.

Bend Brewing Company
1019 NW Brooks St., 541-383-1599
bendbrewingco.com

Waypoint
921 NW Mt. Washington Dr.
waypointbbc.com

BECOME A WINE CONNOISSEUR
AT A LOCAL TASTING ROOM OR WINERY

Beer might be king in the Pacific Northwest, but we also make great wine. Pinot noir is probably Oregon's most popular contribution to the wine world, but vineyards in the state are said to produce almost 100 varieties of grapes. Plenty of these varieties are ready to be appreciated in the many tasting rooms around town. And though most grapes are cultivated on the west side of the Cascades, daring winemakers have also been able to grow in the tougher climates of Central Oregon. Props to Lava Terrace for attempting this difficult deed first in Bend. Find their wines at Elixir Wine Group and other shops around town. Faith, Hope & Charity Vineyards is another popular vineyard at the top of the game. Nestled between two ridges and a canyon in Terrebonne on over 300 acres, they offer winery tours, live music, and other events, including weddings, year-round. It takes unrelenting determination to challenge the climate of the high desert, and these vintners are proving successful.

Faith, Hope & Charity Vineyards
70450 Lower Valley Dr., Terrebonne, 541-526-5075
faithhopeandcharityevents.com

Lava Terrace Cellars
20520 Bowery Ln., 541-280-9935
lavaterracecellars.com

AWAKEN YOUR APPETITE
AT SPARROW BAKERY

Tears poured and the Deschutes nearly overflowed when Bendites heard that Sparrow Bakery was closing its location in the Old Iron Works building. Fear not, because they are still alive and well in Northwest Crossing. And, yes, the tantalizing aromas of freshly baked breads and pastries still permeate the air from open till close. Master bakers mix all the right herbs and spices to satisfy those early morning cravings. Order a slice of carrot cake or banana bread that is so moist it will melt in your mouth. Try the Bendfamous Ocean Roll, a croissant roll made with cardamom, sugar, and vanilla. If you have a larger appetite for breakfast or brunch, Sparrow has several signature sandwiches and soups. Can't make it to their side of town? They deliver!

2748 NW Crossing, #110, 541-647-2323
thesparrowbakery.net

PLEASE YOUR PALATE
AT DRAKE

When first walking into Drake you get the look and feel of a retro diner. But stay awhile, view the menu, and the atmosphere of this downtown restaurant begins to feel more upscale. The server greets you with a bag of the house popcorn, full of flavor and whetting your appetite. Since the restaurant always finds ways to be innovative and add to the menu, you may want to try the daily special or ask for a seasonal dish. My personal favorite, a mainstay on the menu, is the mac and cheese made with white and yellow cheddar. It pops with flavor and is perfect with a local IPA. For lunch or dinner, Drake is a great choice, right in the heart of everything, and a good way to begin or end a trip downtown.

801 NW Wall St., 541-306-3366
drakebend.com

EMBRACE THE DECADENCE
AT DANDY'S DRIVE-IN

In most cities, arguments constantly ensue about which restaurant has the best burgers, the best pizza, the best hot wings—the list goes on. Bend is no exception. And while it might be impossible to get every single person to agree on the tastiest burger (or anything, for that matter), most of them will likely put Dandy's Drive-In at the top of the list. A staple in the community for years, Dandy's is one of those places where you get anxious while waiting for the server to skate up to the car. Your belly may start to growl while patiently waiting for the big, juicy, mouthwatering burger with a side of tater tots. Go all out and order the Double Grand Dandy or keep it simple with a namesake Dandy Burger and fries. Oh, and be sure to save room for one of their signature milkshakes or floats.

1334 NE 3rd St., 541-382-6141
dandysdrivein.com

INDULGE IN HAPPY HOUR
AT THE ICONIC PINE TAVERN

The most iconic restaurant in Bend has something you don't see every day in a dining room: two giant ponderosa pines growing through the roof! Over 80 years old, the Pine Tavern was originally opened in the 1930s by two enterprising women to serve the growing timber industry's workers and their families. The restaurant has gained a reputation as a must-visit destination in Bend for a number of reasons. The food is exceptional, the view overlooking Mirror Pond is breathtaking, and the bar is often voted the best happy hour in Bend. Over the years, Pine Tavern has evolved and morphed to keep pace with the times, and the establishment looks like it will be around for another 80 years. Be sure to try the sourdough scones with honey butter when you visit.

967 NW Brooks St., 541-382-5581
pinetavern.com

ABSORB THE SUNSET
AT CRUX FERMENTATION

Imagine a panoramic view of the sun setting behind the Cascade Mountains in a large, comfortable courtyard. The kids are playing. You are surrounded by friends or family. No need to cook or clean up, yet you have a wide variety of food and drink available. Sound too good to be true? At Crux Fermentation Project dreams become reality. The brewery has a taproom with a seemingly endless choice of unique brews and a food menu that promises to please. And just to give us more choice, the courtyard has food carts set up as well. For a little extra love and to make the sunset even more magical, every day Crux celebrates the "Sundowner Hour" with discounts on food and drink. Dreams really do come true.

50 SW Division St., 541-385-3333
cruxfermentation.com

EAT LOCAL
WITH CENTRAL OREGON LOCAVORE

The folks at Central Oregon Locavore know how to have a good time. Promoting the farm-to-table lifestyle, their goal is to raise awareness about eating locally, healthily, and sustainably. They often do so in the most entertaining way possible. Local chefs, restaurants, and farms collaborate to offer culinary-related classes and events. Why not learn a Bollywood dance while trying a delicious feast of Indian cuisine? Surely you have been wanting to learn how to make handmade tortillas from the chefs at the local Mexican restaurant. Have you ever met and eaten with the farmer of the savory meal you are enjoying? Seriously, after learning about this place, I feel I can become a culinary master. More importantly, I am getting schooled on the importance of eating locally. If you can't attend one of the events, stop by the marketplace and pick up some fresh, locally farmed and grown food.

1841 NE 3rd St., 541-633-7388
centraloregonlocavore.org

FINE DINE FROM A–Z
IN BEND

Whether they know it or not, two restaurants seem to be in constant competition with each other to win local palates in Bend: Ariana and Zydeco. Both have exquisite dishes, so it really depends on your taste and your mood. But why not enjoy both? Zydeco Kitchen & Cocktails is where the Pacific Northwest meets the South. Not many places serve up tasty baby back ribs and redfish on the same menu. Ariana has its own take on the Pacific Northwest and fuses it with a Mediterranean style. Indulge yourself with the Chef's Tasting Menu, currently a six-course tour that will leave you blissfully satisfied. No two restaurants are alike, and with either of these you cannot go wrong. Be sure to try both, just not on the same night.

Ariana
1304 NW Galveston Ave., 541-330-5539
arianarestaurantbend.com

Zydeco Kitchen & Cocktails
919 NW Bond St., 541-312-2899
zydecokitchen.com

FILL UP ON DELECTABLE PIZZA PIES
AROUND TOWN

Like many people, pizza tops the list of my favorite foods. A cook and delivery driver during my younger years, I basically used to live on cheesy pizza pies. These days, I often make them from scratch at home and frequently eat at one of the local vendors. I know a good pizza. In Bend, Pizza Mondo has won the readers' choice "Best Of" for over 20 years, and no doubt they offer some of the most delectable pies in town. Luckily, for aficionados like me who crave variety, as the city grows, so do our pizza choices. Abe Capanna's Detroit Style, Rush Squares, and Fratelli Pies are among those that have recently entered the scene. These are a few of my favorites, but many more in Central Oregon are worth a try as well. I'm getting hungry just writing this. Gotta go!

Abe Capanna's
566 SW Mill View Way, 541-390-3285
8handshospitality.com

Fratelli Pies
1227 NW Galveston Ave., Ste. B, 541-241-4272
fratellipies.com

Pizza Mondo
811 NW Wall St., 541-330-9093
pizzamondobend.com

Rush's Squares
1424 NE Cushing Dr., 541-706-0653
rushssquares.com

TREAT YOURSELF TO AN EARLY MORNING DRINK
AT MCKAY COTTAGE

Tradition says it's never too early to drink a Bloody Mary or mimosa. Some people would even argue it's a healthy way to start the day. I mean, the drinks do have fruit juice and all, right? McKay Cottage Restaurant is known as the hot spot for breakfast in Bend, and not only because of the morning libations. A menu full of favorites like the Gourmet Breakfast Sandwich and the Oatmeal Pancakes are the perfect way to start the day off right. Mornings can often be a bit chilly around town, but the staff at McKay Cottage will offer you blankets if you decide to sit outside. Some tables have fire pits to keep you warm. After your belly is full, you may choose to go across the street to Sawyer Park for a quiet walk along the river. I can't think of a better way to begin the day.

62910 O.B. Riley Rd., 541-383-2697
themckaycottage.com

JOIN
THE KOMBUCHA CRAZE

After reading this far, you probably think that beer is the only beverage in Bend. Not so. Rapidly gaining popularity is kombucha, sometimes called the nectar of the gods. A type of fermented tea, many people enjoy the taste, while others point to the health benefits. Either way, if you haven't tried the drink before, a world of new flavors awaits, from sweet coconut lime to spicy lemon ginger. Stores around the country carry kombucha, but here in Bend tons of local restaurants have it on tap. And if you want to go straight to the source, where it's freshest, stop at the Humm Kombucha taproom, one of the largest, most innovative brewers in the country. Here you can mix and match and try as many flavors as you like. You may end up with a new favorite drink.

Humm Kombucha
1125 NE 2nd St., 541-306-6329
hummkombucha.com

GET A HOPPY EDUCATION
ON A DESCHUTES BREWERY TOUR

Founded in 1988, Deschutes Brewery holds the title as the oldest brewery in Bend. It is also one of the largest craft breweries in the entire country. The production facility on the Deschutes River is ginormous, and on windy days when they are brewing, the smell of hops permeates the air for a mile or more away. Lucky for you, the facility offers tours. Before the tour starts, the guide offers a cold, canned beverage. Then, in a little less than an hour, you will make your way through halls of hops, giant steel vats full of wort, futuristic-looking bottling machines, and every other step of the beer-making process. By then, your beer will probably be empty, and you'll want to try one of the other types of brews the tour guide mentioned. Mosey on down to the taproom, taste as many as you like, and order a favorite.

901 SW Simpson Ave., 541-385-8606
deschutesbrewery.com/brewery-tour

TIP

Like many events, the Deschutes Brewery tours were affected by the pandemic. The taproom is still regularly open to try some brews, earn a BAT stamp, and purchase cool swag, but be sure to call ahead if your primary purpose is a tour. If numbers are low and regulations relaxed, you can bet they will be proudly showing off the inner workings of the brewery.

MUSIC
AND ENTERTAINMENT

SEE A LIVE SHOW
AT HAYDEN HOMES AMPHITHEATER

During the summer months the big names come to Bend: Nine Inch Nails, Luke Bryan, Black Crowes, and Alice in Chains, to name a few. The Hayden Homes Amphitheater is hands down the best place to see live music in the city. And it's not just the bands. Blue skies slowly giving way to the sunset, the flow of the Deschutes River, a large open grassy area, and an energized crowd all collude to create an electric atmosphere. Even if you cannot attend a show, the sound and enthusiasm carry across much of the city and you can hear the music clearly almost anywhere nearby. When performers aren't onstage, the amphitheater still hosts festivals and other events. Even during the winter, the grass area is open for all to enjoy, including the hundreds (maybe thousands) of Canadian geese that flock to the area.

344 SW Shevlin Hixon Dr., 541-318-5457
bendconcerts.com

TIP

When the holiday season arrives, Santa Claus flies to Bend by helicopter! He uses the open grass field at the amphitheater as a landing pad. Rain, shine, or heavy snow, it's a sight to see. Be sure to take the kids, who usually rush to him after he steps out and starts passing out candy and hugs.

WAKE UP EARLY
FOR BALLOONS OVER BEND

During the third weekend in July, the early bird catches the worm. Why? At dawn, giant, colorful hot-air balloons are launched into the sky during the Balloons Over Bend Festival! Friday through Sunday the daring pilots take off in their balloons from Bend and float around Central Oregon. Then the party begins! Hosted by the Central Oregon Community College Foundation, the event promises a fun-filled weekend with obstacle courses for kids, live music, a marketplace, and other exciting entertainment. Each day's events culminate into the Night Glow, when the pilots inflate their balloons to give everyone a glow in the dark, magical experience. The city of Redmond hosts one day of parties as well. Keep your eyes open over the weekend because the skies will be more colorful than usual.

Lay It Out Events
541-323-0964
balloonsoverbend.com

LET THE KIDS (AND ADULTS) CUT LOOSE
AT SUN MOUNTAIN FUN CENTER

Bend has plenty of places for kids to cut loose, but only one spot has a good mix of everything. Whether celebrating a birthday, a special occasion, or a family fun day out, Sun Mountain Fun Center has been keeping people entertained since the mid-90s. Younger children can enjoy bumper cars, the arcade, or the carnival ride. Older kids can have friendly competitions on the go-karts, play Laser Tag, skee-ball, mini-golf, and more. Adults, don't think you are too old to experience the excitement. Show the family your bowling skills, exercise those arms in the batting cage, play billiards, or immerse yourself in virtual reality. No matter what age, when it's time to get some energy out and play, Sun Mountain Fun Center is where the fun always shines!

300 Bend River Mall Dr., 541-382-6161
sunmountainfun.com

TEST YOUR ENDURANCE
AT OREGON WINTERFEST

Oregonians are a hardy breed, and whatever the weather, they know how to party! In fact, they throw a huge three-day festival on some of the coldest days of the year. WinterFest, held in February, celebrates a time of year when most people prefer to be inside next to a cozy fireplace. Not in Central Oregon! Like most festivals, plenty of food and drink tents are available. Kids' activities and local vendors are abundant. Musicians play throughout the weekend, and you can't miss the dog shows. But what really sets WinterFest apart from other festivals are the friendly competitions. Seeing the intricately carved ice sculptures alone is worth the price of admission. The custom-built firepits not only keep you warm, but they are truly works of art, especially when they come alive at dark. With so much entertainment, you may forget how cold it is outside!

Deschutes County Expo Center, 541-323-0964
oregonwinterfest.com

BECOME A TRUE FILM BUFF
AT BENDFILM FESTIVAL

The Avengers, Star Wars, Wedding Crashers—those movies are decent and all, but most of the best films being created are independent. Rated the best film festival in the Pacific Northwest, the annual BendFilm Festival gives you an opportunity to see some of these high-quality indie films. Always more intimate, for four days during the fall you get the chance to meet and engage the actors, directors, and others involved in the movie, not to mention four days' worth of parties! Growing bigger by the year, nine screens in Central Oregon showcase films from around the world. If you stick to the big, cookie-cutter blockbuster movies you really can't consider yourself a movie buff, but after attending this festival you will have a fresh perspective and appreciation for quality film.

1000 NW Wall St., Ste. 240, 541-388-FEST
bendfilm.org

TIP

Have a future moviemaker in the family?
BendFilm is deeply involved in the community.
The BendFilm Future Filmmakers competitions
gives kids in 5th–12th grade the opportunity to
display their talents and learn their craft better.
Prizes are awarded and, most importantly, kids
get to interact with other filmmakers, get
recognized, and hone their skills.

MAKE MAGICAL MEMORIES
WITH WANDERLUST TOURS

Wanderlust Tours offers the most creative, fun, and memorable experiences one can imagine. From the novice to the pro, from local breweries to remote areas of Steens Mountain Wilderness, the company truly has something for everyone to enjoy. Kayak on one of the Cascade lakes in summer. Explore a lava tube cave in spring or snow camp in winter. Many tours are available year-round, others by season, but for an extra meaningful experience, take one of the specialty tours. Can you picture spending Valentine's under the bright stars of the night sky as you snowshoe to a bonfire with alcohol-infused hot cocoa or espresso waiting? Enjoying the acoustics of a local a cappella group during a concert in an 80,000-year-old cave? Sounds pretty amazing, right? These are a few of the many experiences Wanderlust takes to a new level.

61535 S Hwy. 97, Ste. 13, 541-389-8359
wanderlusttours.com

TIP

So many people visiting and moving to Central Oregon has an impact. And while most individuals respect the environment, those bad apples still exist. Wanderlust Tours attempts to mitigate these negative effects through their Voluntourism program. Volunteers help remove graffiti from caves and pick up trash in important areas. Every little bit we do to curb the problem helps, especially when we all contribute. Consider joining one of these helpful events.

CATCH A PERFORMANCE
AT TOWER THEATRE

You would never guess that the iconic Tower Theatre began as a cafeteria opened by the same ladies who went on to create the Pine Tavern. Over the years, the building has changed hands often and even been closed down a few times. But now, thanks to a caring community, the large bright neon lights make the venue one of Bend's most prized and recognizable destinations. The theater has been beautifully renovated to create an amazingly intimate and comfortable experience for the performers and their audiences. As host to 220+ activities a year, you can bet there is something for everyone—Celtic, rock, and mariachi concerts; musicals and plays; films; nature nights; weddings; presentations—the list goes on. Often called Bend's Living Room, Tower Theatre sits at the apex of the city's cultural vibe.

835 NW Wall St., 541-317-0700
towertheatre.org

SHOWCASE YOUR USELESS KNOWLEDGE
ON TRIVIA NIGHTS

How smart are you and your friends? Care to wager a drink or two on it? If so, grab your most intelligent crew, create a silly team name, and get ready for an entertaining evening with Useless Knowledge Bowl Trivia! Kevin, the MC and quizmaster, hosts the fun at venues all around Bend and Redmond almost every night of the week. Did someone say drink specials? Another reason to go! Trivia categories range from sports to popular culture to literature and everything in between. Questions, mostly multiple choice, are presented vividly on screens with extra chances for bonus points at the end of rounds. Winners walk away with prizes and bragging rights. Losers, if nothing else, get cheaper drinks and a fun time. More than your average trivia night, everybody participating in UKB Trivia will leave a bit smarter!

All around Bend and Redmond
ukbtrivia.com

RIDE THROUGH BEND IN STYLE
WITH WHEEL FUN RENTALS

Walking to a destination can sometimes take too long, and when driving you often miss the blissful surroundings. Plus, who wants to find a place to park, especially during the busy tourist season? Biking is the best way to do Bend. Wheel Fun Rentals has everything from eight passenger Surreys to tandem bicycles, multi-speed bikes, baby joggers, and the regular two-wheeled bikes most of us are accustomed to. Go wherever you like during the rental time or take the self-guided bicycle tour. Ask for the map, which gives detailed directions and brief explanations about some of the best destinations in town. The route passes through McKay Park, the Deschutes River Trail, Mirror Pond, and more. A few food suggestions are also included, but we like to pack a lunch and have a picnic in one of the parks on the route.

603 SW Mill View Way, 541-408-4568
wheelfunrentals.com/or/bend/old-mill-district

CHILL OUTSIDE
DURING MUNCH & MUSIC

Summer in Bend has arrived. The weather is perfect. Everyone is happy and ready to spend every waking moment outside. On Thursday evenings during July and August, the place to be is Drake Park for free music. Better known as Munch & Music, an outdoor amphitheater backs up to the river, and the sweet melodies liven up the mood and make everyone ecstatic. Grab yourself a low-back chair or blanket and share the grassy area with friends or complete strangers. You'll make friends soon enough. Local artisans have tents set up to sell their wares and of course there will be plenty of food trucks to appease your appetite. There may even be a bouncy house or two to wear out the kiddos. Family-friendly fun for all, and an amazing way to spend a Thursday evening.

Drake Park
777 NW Riverside Blvd.
munchandmusic.com

FEEL THE MUSIC
AT VOLCANIC THEATRE PUB

And I do mean feel the music, as it reverberates through your body. A concert at Volcanic Theatre Pub in Bend is about as up close and personal as you can get. This large area has the perfect amount of space for live shows, with plenty of room to dance and move around or lounge on cozy sofas, recliners, and other seating. VTP mostly hosts local and national musicians, but you'll also see an eclectic mix of other types of performances. One visit might feel like a rambunctious party and the next like a chill evening with friends. Watch a standup comedian when you need a little laughter, see a live theater show if you're in a cerebral mood, relax and watch a movie, or just take the family and enjoy the positive vibes.

70 SW Century Dr., 541-323-1881
volcanictheatre.com

UNLEASH YOUR INNER PHOTOGRAPHER
WITH BEND PHOTO TOURS

These days, smart phones and affordable digital cameras allow everyone the chance to snap great pics. I know I like to think I'm a decent photographer. But true photography is an art with many technicalities to be learned. The talented crew at Bend Photo Tours will help sharpen your skills and teach the artistic aspects of taking amazing pictures. The company offers year-round guided tours, workshops, presentations, and personalized tutoring for the novice to the expert. Capture the Cascades by helicopter, snap Sahalie Falls surrounded by snow, or choose your own expedition. What better way to boost your abilities and learn the intricacies of photography than through hands-on adventures among the limitless beauty of Central Oregon? We all want that perfect photo to hang on the wall or post on Instagram. After a Bend Photo Tour, all your pictures will be worthy of framing.

541-640-1089
bendphototours.com

RELIVE YOUR YOUTH
AT VECTOR VOLCANO ARCADE

Heart racing, hands sweating, blood pumping—all the excitement will make you feel like a kid again at Vector Volcano. A blast from the past, I thought I had grown out of gaming until I saw the well-kept arcade games from the '80s and '90s like Pac-Man, Kung-Fu Master, Galaga, Mortal Kombat, Frogger, and other favorites. The arcade has an area up front with pinball machines that take coins to play. In the same area, you can purchase drinks. Beyond the front, pay by the hour and get limitless play on all the other games. Introducing the classics of my childhood to my daughters was just as much fun, and they thought I was some kind of ninja master until they saw me get beat by another guy my age in Street Fighter II.

111 NW Oregon Ave.
vectorvolcanoarcade.com

SUPPORT LIVE THEATER
AT THOROUGHLY MODERN PRODUCTIONS

For a smaller town, Bend is bursting with talent, and at Thoroughly Modern Productions the talent comes alive through live performances on stage. TMP helps kids interested in stagecraft develop new theater skills and follow their passions. Working alongside experienced adults, they can learn acting, dancing, singing, set designing, and stage managing. Whether performing in front of an audience or working behind the scenes, there is a place for everyone interested in the performing arts. Even if you don't have children, I suggest watching a live production, often performed at the iconic Tower Theatre. Popular versions of musicals and plays like *The Wizard of Oz*, *Annie*, *Legally Blonde*, and *My Son Pinocchio Jr.*, will pleasantly surprise you. Plus, the courage and hard work of these actors deserve praise. I wish I had the guts to get onstage!

541-679-0313
facebook.com/thoroughlymodernproductions

DISCOVER
THE SECRET ROOMS
OF MCMENAMINS

McMenamins has an unconventional flavor like no other place in Bend. Once St. Francis Catholic School, the building is now home to a restaurant, a hotel, a brewery, a Turkish hot pool, and don't tell anyone—secret rooms. The rooms are not difficult to find, but take the long way so you can savor the experience of this unique establishment. First, enter through the restaurant and admire the exotic art from all over the world scattered about. Then, pass through the hall of the main hotel to glimpse the history of the school. The spirit of St. Francis School stays alive through the artwork, photos, and other memorabilia that adorn the walls. Once outside, cross the parking lot to enter a courtyard. Pass O'Kanes, the cigar room, and you will see two newer buildings, both hotels. Go inside the one named the Art Room. Now we can search for the secret rooms (and again don't tell anyone). On the first floor, search for a hidden entrance that takes you to a blacklight room reminiscent of *Alice in Wonderland*. Stop awhile, and if the room is not full of teenagers making TikTok videos, snap pics of your own. The hidden entrance on the second floor will lead to a room with chalkboard walls full of aphorisms, autographs, and scribbled art. Leave your mark. On the third floor, search for the Broom Closet, which from the outside looks like a storage room for Quidditch broomsticks. Step inside and you have entered a small and cozy speakeasy. Time to reward yourself with a drink for finding the mysterious three secret rooms.

700 NW Bond St., 541-382-5174
mcmenamins.com/old-st-francis-school

TIP

Do you like collecting stuff, or in this case, experiences? McMenamins has its own passport available. Get it stamped at each eclectic location (over 50 around the Pacific Northwest) and earn food, merchandise, concert tickets, and even lodging. These places are amazingly awesome!

IGNITE YOUR CREATIVITY
AT 9TH STREET VILLAGE

What started as the DIY Cave has quickly grown into the largest creative environment in Bend. A giant maker space, this is the ideal area to let your creative juices flow or to learn new skills. Classes for all ages teach how to work with metal, wood, paint, and more. An outdoor "tiny home build" space can be rented and allows for massive projects. Since its inception, the area has expanded to become the 9th Street Village and currently includes a skate shop, (SOLSK8S), a coffee shop (Industrial Joes), a food truck lot, and Bevel Brewing. When your imagination exhausts itself or needs a break, grab a drink and a snack, and mingle with other likeminded creatives. Truly living up to its name as a village, everything you need is on-site.

DIY Cave
444 SE 9th St., #150, 541-388-2283
diycave.com

SOLSK8S
484 SE 9th St., #150, 541-797-7616
seedoflifeskateboards.com

Bevel Brewing
911 SE Armour Rd., Ste. B
541-973-3835
bevelbeer.com

Industrial Joes Coffee
541-280-4862
facebook.com/industrialjoescoffee

WITNESS THE JULY 4TH PET PARADE
BEFORE WATCHING FIREWORKS

Pets, especially dogs, have the best life in Bend. They are treated like children, maybe better. In fact, Bend has been named one of the "dog friendliest" cities by a number of publications. So, you can bet that on the Fourth of July, the Pet Parade is a sight to behold. Hundreds of animals walk the streets of downtown strutting their stuff and sniffing their friends' backsides. Their owners sometimes pull them in wagons or small bikes, in baby strollers, or small, elaborate floats. Some pets are all dazzled up in snazzy outfits, usually with red, white, and blue for the occasion. Mostly dogs participate, but you may also see horses, lizards, snakes, and possibly even a baby coyote or badger. Don't own a pet? Grab your favorite stuffed animal and be part of the entertainment!

Downtown Bend
bendparksandrec.org/activities/4th-of-july-festival

GET A BLAST FROM THE PAST
AT THE LAST BLOCKBUSTER

Once an empire with thousands of stores, Blockbuster Video now has one last physical location in the entire world. And, yes, the city of Bend is lucky enough to claim it! A documentary about the store, a TV show, an opportunity to spend the night as an Airbnb—the Last Blockbuster has morphed into a cultural icon. Stop by and it is normal to see tourists posing for selfies in front of the store and browsing the aisles. Lots of unique mementos can be purchased as souvenirs (including this book!). If nostalgia is not reason enough for a visit, Blockbuster still maintains a large selection of DVDs and Blu-rays, some obscure and difficult to find on streaming services. Fairly priced, too, I might add. In the age of HBO Max, Netflix, and other increasingly overwhelming choices, it is fun to see my kids walk around the store and stare in awe at generations of films. It really makes me appreciate what we used to take for granted. Get a membership card today, true movie aficionados!

211 NE Revere Ave., 541-385-9111
bendblockbuster.com

CUT LOOSE
AT THE DESCHUTES
COUNTY FAIR & RODEO

I'm no cowboy, but that doesn't keep me from having a good time at the Deschutes County Fair & Rodeo. Still going strong after over 100 years, the Deschutes County Expo Center hosts the largest event in Central Oregon for almost a full week in early August. Devour a funnel cake or cotton candy with the kids. Ride the Extreme Scream or tone it down on a carrousel. Visit the prize pigs, goats, and other livestock. Listen to live concerts from both local and well-known musicians. Watch in awe as the true cowboys attempt to ride a bucking horse for eight seconds. And everything I mentioned is just part of the action. With so much entertainment, all ages and all types of people will have a blast. You don't have to be a cowboy to enjoy this ride!

3800 SW Airport Way, Redmond, 541-548-2711
expo.deschutes.org/fair

UNCOVER THE BEST OF CENTRAL OREGON
WITH THE ULTIMATE SCAVENGER

The most adventurous and exciting way to see the many treasures of Central Oregon is on a scavenger hunt. Lucky for you, the Ultimate Scavenger offers year-round hunts and tours for individuals, groups, and businesses. For the competitive types among us, a huge citywide scavenger hunt takes place once a year. Random teams with silly names are cut loose to decipher and act out clues while scouring the city in the allotted time. The first group to complete the hunt with the most points is the Ultimate Scavenger and wins cash money! Other contestants who finish the hunt win cool prizes as well. The hunts are an entertaining and educational way to test your knowledge about the area and discover new things you never knew existed. Sign me up!

Citywide
901-210-5104
facebook.com/ultimatescavenger

TIP

The Ultimate Scavenger offers many entertaining ways to explore Central Oregon. Specific themed hunts for Bend, Redmond, local murals, nature, breweries, and more are always available. Check out the interactive activity books, monthly subscription hunts, and other featured items as well. Plus, when you participate you get a certificate and the opportunity to win other awesome prizes!

bendmarketplace.com/
?s=ultimate+scavenger

SPORTS
AND RECREATION

LEARN TO SNOW SKI OR SNOWBOARD
AT MOUNT BACHELOR

On any clear day in Bend, Mount Bachelor can be seen standing alone and impressively rising above the landscape. This volcano (no worries, it isn't expected to erupt anytime soon) is a winter wonderland for skiing and snowboarding enthusiasts during the snowy months of the year. For beginners like me, it's a chance to learn the difference between downhill and Nordic skiing, and to find out if snowboarding is as impressive as it looks when I watch the Olympics. For those new to skiing, purchase the SKI OR RIDE IN 5 pass, which will get you five lessons from seasoned instructors, but be sure to purchase them early because they sell out quickly. Tickets for the lift and the equipment are included as well, but bring your own warm clothing!

13000 SW Century Dr., 541-382-1709
mtbachelor.com

TIP

Looking for an alternative to Mount Bachelor? Driving a bit farther north past Sisters will get you to the Hoodoo Ski Area, a destination many skiers prefer. A different atmosphere with some awesome ski runs, this might be your new favorite spot. They even offer night skiing!

27400 Big Lake Rd., Sisters, 541-822-3799
skihoodoo.com

FIND PEACE IN THE FOREST
AT SHEVLIN PARK

Not many cities can boast a natural recreation area the size of Shevlin Park. At almost 1,000 acres, the space is an ideal place to escape the city life and rejuvenate in the forest. A small pond near the parking lot is perfect for beginning fisherman or those who want to relax. Tumalo Creek rambles lazily through the park, and most of the trails follow it closely, allowing hikers to stop and listen to the peaceful, flowing water. Have a picnic or take a dip. And while many trails near Bend are covered in snow during the winter months, those at Shevlin Park are usually still accessible. The quaking aspens, ponderosa pines, and other native trees and plants are beautiful year-round and offer a sense of remoteness that make you think you are far away from civilization. You may never want to leave.

18920 NW Shevlin Park Rd.
bendparksandrec.org/park/shevlin-park

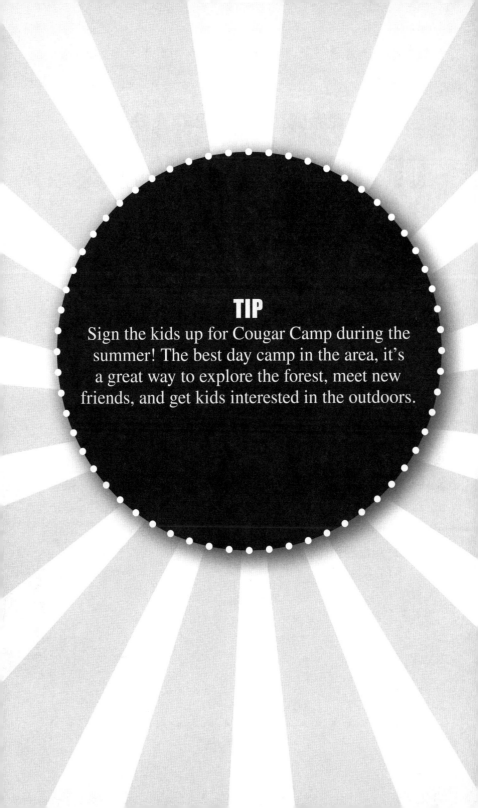

TIP

Sign the kids up for Cougar Camp during the summer! The best day camp in the area, it's a great way to explore the forest, meet new friends, and get kids interested in the outdoors.

HEAR THE ROAR OF THE MIGHTY RAPIDS
AT BENHAM AND DILLON FALLS

All this talk about waterfalls, turquoise blue waters, snowcapped peaks, and other natural phenomena has probably got you thinking Central Oregon is the stuff of dreams. It is, and let me add another worthwhile hike to prove my point. The trek from Benham Falls to Dillon Falls gives some of the most spectacular views of the Deschutes River: towering ponderosas, fields of otherworldly lava rock, wildflowers (in summer), and other native vegetation. All the while the river roars beside you. In fact, the falls are not really waterfalls, but the largest rapids on the Deschutes. If you've hiked the entirety of the Deschutes River Trail you will have passed these points, but since they are a ways out of town, most people drive to them, park, get a glimpse, and return to Bend. Don't just get a taste, walk the trail to get the full meal.

541-383-4000
fs.usda.gov

DIG FOR TREASURES
NEAR BEND

Grab the shovels, goggles, picks, gloves, buckets, and whatever other digging tools you have at home and go rockhounding! You may be asking yourself, what in the world is that? Well, a person who searches for and collects minerals is considered a rockhound. Geologically, Oregon is one of the best places in the US for venturing out to discover distinctive rocks like sunstone, obsidian, agate, petrified wood, and Oregon's state rock—the cool-looking thunderegg. Keeping these rocks is completely legal in many designated public areas. Visit Bend and other outdoor shops around town have maps of nearby rockhounding destinations. Glass Butte, a spot where you can find all types of otherworldly looking, volcanic glass-like obsidian, is a favorite. It's an adventurous, exciting activity for the entire family to enjoy!

United States Forest Service
541-383-4000
fs.usda.gov

BOND WITH NATURE
ON THE DESCHUTES RIVER TRAIL

The Deschutes River Trail is the reason I first fell in love with Bend. Easily accessible from many points around town, within seconds you are surrounded by nature and can hear the peaceful flow of the river, see massive boulders, and smell the sweet scent of pines, juniper, and other native vegetation. The well-traveled trail hugs the river to create a large loop, and the city is steadily finding ways to expand and improve it. Interpretive signs educate about local vegetation, wildlife, and the history of the area. There are plenty of spots to stop and rest or take in the scenery. Perfect for walking or running, the trail is also excellent for getting kids interested in hiking. Farewell Bend and Riverbend Park are my favorite access points to begin.

bendtrails.org/trail/deschutes-river-trail

TIP

Naturally, kids enjoy hiking more when they are having fun. To get them interested in the outdoors and hiking, play games along the trail. Create a scavenger hunt, deputize them rangers, or let them stop along the way to explore. My daughters like to search for fairy holes and build houses for them from whatever they find lying around in the forest. Their imagination runs wild!

SLED LIKE CHEVY CHASE
AT WANOGA SNO-PARK

If you recognize the title reference from the movie *Christmas Vacation*, be prepared to experience the sled ride of your life! At Wanoga Sno-Park there is a huge, steep hill right near the parking lot that screams, "Slide down me!" It's really not difficult to climb and you can go up as far as you like, the farther, the faster. Then, yell with nervous glee as you sled uncontrollably down the hill at a hundred miles an hour. Not really, but it feels fast and it's more exhilarating than a ride at the amusement park. But be careful! On crowded days, not everyone has sense enough to get out of the way, and it is difficult to stop once you get started. Smaller hills are strewn around the park as well for younger kids and those who might want to practice first before going all out.

Cascade Lakes Highway
541-383-4000
fs.usda.gov

TIP

Sleds can be purchased at several hardware stores or retailers around Bend, and in fact, you may want to get one off season. We tried three stores before we found ours because the others were sold out! Spend a few extra bucks and purchase a quality-made sled. Otherwise, you may end up breaking the cheap plastic one on your second slide like I did. And please be sure to take your sled home with you, even it if breaks.
Pack in, pack out.

WITNESS THE MAJESTY OF BIG RED
AT LAPINE STATE PARK

At around 500 years old, 162 feet tall, and with an 8.6 feet diameter, Big Red is the largest ponderosa pine in Oregon! The famed tree was here long before us and hopefully will survive long after. Unfortunately, due to the passage of time, weather, and people who try to climb and vandalize it, the Old Man shows his age. A fence has been built around the tree for protection, but you can still snap a pic and show this mighty conifer your respect. Located in LaPine State Park, Big Red is not the only thing to experience while you're there. The area has plenty of trails for biking, hiking, running, or horse rides. The Deschutes River flows peacefully through the park, with day-use areas for swimming, floating, or kayaking. Rarely overcrowded, it's a perfect place to play.

LaPine State Park
800-551-6949
stateparks.oregon.gov

TURN INTO AN ICICLE
AT TAMOLITCH BLUE POOL

It's a sweltering day. A fun but exhausting hike through the forest along the McKenzie River has you sweating. But then, after a few miles on the trail, you arrive at the destination and are overwhelmed by the beautiful turquoise color of the water. You have arrived at the Tamolitch Blue Pool, one of the most stunning wonders of Central Oregon. Even at a chilly 37 degrees, the pool is definitely worth a swim, or at least a quick dip. Few people last long or get more than their feet wet. Still, the views of the rushing falls and the contrasting reflection of surrounding alders and evergreens on the water make you want to stick around and relish nature at its finest. The color of the water will linger in your mind long after your trip.

National Forest Rd. 2672-655, McKenzie Bridge, 541-383-4000
fs.usda.gov

TIP
Careful! About the time the pool becomes visible you will be overlooking it from atop of a 70-foot ledge and may be tempted to jump. Even though the water can be up to 30 feet deep in some places, jumping from the cliff can be dangerous and people often get hurt, either from the jump or from the surprise of the frigid water! Best just to take a dip at the bottom.

HEAR THE MIGHTY ROAR
OF STEELHEAD FALLS

Tumalo Falls is the highest waterfall near Bend, but Steelhead Falls might be the most scenic. A short, half-mile hike takes you to the falls where there is plenty of space to picnic, fish, or just sit, watch, and listen to the powerful falls roaring over the boulders. You can stop there and be satisfied with the natural beauty of the world, but I suggest hiking the four-mile loop that steadily climbs up to the ridge and offers views of the Cascade peaks. Surrounded by cliffs millions of years old, you get a sense of appreciation for the world and feel lucky to be part of it. Take a rest and breathe in the crisp, fresh air. On the return route, you will probably want to stop at the falls once more to take in their beauty before returning to civilization. Take your time, relax, and plan another hike like this one in the near future.

SW River Rd., Terrebonne, 541-416-6700
blm.gov/visit/steelhead-falls-trail

PREPARE TO
BE AWESTRUCK
AT CRATER LAKE NATIONAL PARK

If you are anywhere near Bend, Crater Lake National Park should not be missed. About a two-hour drive away, this amazing destination is one of the most amazing spots in the US, and, thus, I had to include it on the list. Formed thousands of years ago from climactic volcanic eruptions, the deepest lake in the US has a mesmerizing "crater blue" color that you will never see anywhere else. Take the Rim Drive around the caldera that allows multiple scenic viewpoints of the lake. Explore further by walking the numerous short trails leading to even more astounding views. If you really want to witness the best the area has to offer, camp for a night or two and hike the longer trails. However you choose to visit Oregon's only national park, this destination should be a priority on your bucket list.

Crater Lake, 541-594-3000
nps.gov/crla/index.htm

FISH THE PLENTIFUL WATERS
OF CENTRAL OREGON

Whether you want to relax on the bank of a stream or battle the toughest of fish species, Bend and the surrounding area is a true fisherman's paradise. The rivers, streams, lakes, and ponds are plentiful and pristine. Trout are the most popular, but you can also catch bass and other prized species when you cast your line. Younger and novice fishermen may want to begin at Shevlin Pond or Bend Pine Nursery Pond, two great places to practice and develop skills. Many seasoned anglers fish the Crooked River for its scenery and the Metolius River for the challenge. Fly fishing is exciting to learn, and once you know how to tie a fly accurately you will be hooked, but luckily not like the fish!

Shevlin Pond in Shevlin Park
18920 NW Shevlin Park Rd.
bendparksandrec.org/parks-trails/fishing

Bend Pine Nursery Pond in Bend Pine Park
3750 NE Purcell Blvd.

TIP

Be sure to check the regulations (permits, limits, etc.) before setting out to fish. Not only is this the right thing to do to preserve the aquatic life, but it might also save you from paying a fine later!

TAKE
THE PAULINA PLUNGE

What is the Paulina Plunge, you ask. Well, it's a full day of exciting fun, but let me tell you more. A tour guide shuttles spirited groups of participants into the Oregon backcountry. Once in the midst of the scenic Paulina Mountains, it's time to descend about 2,000 feet back close to where you started. You get a fat-tire bike for the exhilarating downhill journey. Meanwhile, the guide shares stories about the local indigenous people and the saga of Chief Paulina. Even more thrilling are the stops along the way. Several waterfalls break up the ride so you can park the bikes, soak up the views, and take a dip in the cool water. Two of the falls are natural waterslides, where most of the group will be jumping from boulders into the pristine pools. It's the perfect mix of physical activity and laid-back fun.

53750 US-97, La Pine, 541-389-0562
paulinaplunge.com

GET YOUR SURF ON
AT BEND WHITEWATER PARK

The closest ocean to Bend is about a three-hour drive, but this doesn't stop some surf enthusiasts from catching some serious waves. At Bend Whitewater Park, the Deschutes River has been transformed into three passageways. The first passage is a habitat channel to protect river health and wildlife. The second passage is for those who are floating the river. And, yes, the third passage is a whitewater channel that allows seasoned surfers and kayakers to practice their craft! Onlookers can watch with awe from Colombia Street Bridge or McKay Park. Those with enough audaciousness and experience can get out on the whitewater channel and join the fun. Even on the coldest days of winter you may see hardcore surfers in their wetsuits trying to catch that perfect wave!

166 SW Shevlin Hixon Dr., 541-389-7275
bendparksandrec.org/facility/bend-whitewater-park

FLOAT OR PADDLEBOARD
THE DESCHUTES RIVER

Cutting through the center of town, the Deschutes River remains nearly pristine and truly is the lifeline of Bend. The stretch between Farewell Bend Park and Mirror Pond is one of the most popular spots to float, especially on a hot, sweltering day. Not too fast, not too slow, the river flows the perfect speed to allow a gentle, laid-back experience as you pass through the Old Mill, soak up the sun, and stare at the surrounding Cascades. Purchase an innertube, an air mattress, or paddleboard (basically anything that floats) if you plan to get on the river often. Chances are strong that the trip will become a summer ritual. You can also rent from outfitters like Tumalo Creek Kayak & Canoe or Sun Country Tours. Once you disembark at Drake Park you can catch a shuttle that returns to River Bend Park, the most popular launch area, where you can start all over again.

Tumalo Creek Kayak & Canoe
805 SW Industrial Way, 541-317-9407
tumalocreek.com

Sun Country Tours
541 SW 13th St., 541-382-1709
suncountrytours.com

WORK THOSE LEG MUSCLES
AT PHIL'S TRAILHEAD

When I was a kid, I dreamed of competing in the X Games. Life happened, and there were hardly any good biking trails where I lived and so the dream slowly faded. Then, when I moved to Bend and discovered Phil's Trailhead, the fire was rekindled. According to many local bikers, Phil's has the reputation for the best biking around Central Oregon. With roughly 60 miles of trails, the area hosts something for all skill levels. Veteran riders can endure the brutal uphill climbs, roots, rocks, and other obstacles. Novices can slowly work their way up to those more exhilarating technical rides like the COD. For now, I'll stick to the mostly flat but fun Phil's–Ben's Loop. But keep an eye out for my name at the 2025 X Games!

bendtrails.org/trail/phils-trail-complex

TAKE YOURSELF OUT TO THE BALLGAME
WITH THE BEND ELKS

Bend may not have a professional sports team, but that doesn't stop fans from adamantly supporting local amateur baseball. The Bend Elks play June through August at Vince Genna Stadium, so during the summer months it's all about hot dogs, peanuts, and sodas while you spend the afternoon watching America's favorite pastime! Baseball has a long history in Bend, and a number of teams have played in town going back decades. In fact, here's a quick fun fact. Kurt Russell, the well-known actor, once played for the Bend Rainbows, a previous Bend baseball team. The Elks have been playing in the West Coast Baseball League since 2000. After participating in all the endless outdoor activities around here, I find it nice to sit back, relax, and be a spectator. Take me out to the ballgame!

Vince Genna Stadium
401 SE Roosevelt Ave., 541-312-9259
bendelks.com

DRIVE
THE PICTURESQUE CASCADE LAKES SCENIC BYWAY

It would take more than a lifetime to fully explore the area surrounding Bend, but a perfect place to start is the Cascade Lakes Scenic Byway. You will be awed from just taking a day trip and driving the scenic road through the mountains without ever leaving the car. Better yet, stop at a few of the 14 alpine lakes, get your feet wet, or snap some photos of the Cascade Mountains reflected in the crystal-clear waters. Maybe watch a sunset or have a picnic. You can also view at least 16 interpretive sites along the highway that were selected because of conservation education, gorgeous views, and access to the Deschutes River and Cascade Lakes. Most likely, you will feel the urge to return and dive deeper into this majestic area.

traveloregon.com/things-to-do/trip-ideas/scenic-drives/
cascades-lakes-scenic-byway

TIP

To really enjoy and submerge yourself in the miracle of this area, you should visit one lake at a time and spend a day (or more) there. Every lake has distinct features, whether it's Hosmer Lake for fishing, Elk Lake for swimming, or Sparks Lake for peaceful kayaking. Most locals have a favorite. And although the lakes are most popular during the summer, with the change of seasons comes a change of scenery worth checking out. However, the road closes due to snow during the winter months so plan accordingly.

STAY ACTIVE DURING WINTER
AT THE PAVILION

Bendites love their winter sports, and you can bet that if it's not cold or snowy enough to play outside, they will go to the Pavilion to satisfy their urges. This state-of-the-art facility has a huge NHL-size sheet of ice, perfect for sliding and gliding. But that's not all. Ever tried curling? Me either, but after seeing how much fun folks were having while playing, I plan to try it. Take ice skating classes, join a curling league, play on a hockey team, or just drop by for an open skate. Even as a spectator, you can keep warm in the viewing room or at a firepit outside. And don't think the Pavilion sits idle during the summer. They offer sports camps, roller skating, dodgeball, and classes galore!

1001 SW Bradbury Dr., 541-389-7588
bendparksandrec.org/facility/the-pavilion

STROLL
THROUGH DRAKE PARK

How about an idyllic stroll along the scenic Mirror Pond? Have a quiet picnic? Let the kids or the dog run around and play? Meet up for a bike ride with friends? Read the interpretive signs to learn more about Bend's history? You can do all this and more at Drake Park. The acres of open lawn, striking views of the water, and proximity to downtown make this park a favorite in Bend. During spring and summer, all sorts of festivals and events take place, like Munch & Music and the Fourth of July celebration after the Pet Parade. During winter, enjoy breathtaking views of the snow-covered park while the kids sled the hills. If you are lucky, you may spot one of the great horned owls that make the park home. If not, you will most definitely see a Canadian goose or a thousand.

777 NW Riverside Blvd.
bendparksandrec.org/park/drake-park-and-mirror-pond

SIGN UP FOR A HIKE OR WALK
WITH THE DESCHUTES LAND TRUST

So much to know about nature, and the more I play outside, the stronger my thirst to learn. The Deschutes Land Trust holds informative events throughout the year to educate those of us interested in the outdoors. The trust is a nonprofit run significantly on donations and the help of volunteers with a mission to conserve and protect lands in Central Oregon. My favorite events are the numerous walks and hikes offered during the year. Each is geared toward a particular topic like bird or wildflower identification, geology, and even a hike that gives tips about nature journaling. Others, like the butterfly walk, are ideal for kids. Virtual events are also available. I may never know everything there is to know about the Central Oregon wilderness, but every time I explore the nature preserves with outdoor experts, I feel a bit more knowledgeable.

210 NW Irving Ave., Ste. 102, 541-330-0017
deschuteslandtrust.org

VIEW THE CASCADES
OF TUMALO FALLS

The tallest, most photogenic waterfall in Central Oregon is right in Bend's backyard. Tumalo Falls roars over a cliff nearly 100 feet high. Imagine that power slowly wearing the large boulders down to pebbles over millions of years. To me, it's insanely remarkable. For instant gratification, snap your photos at the viewpoint where most people stop, literally feet from the parking lot. To explore more beauty, follow the trail upward to countless other smaller cascades and a grand view from the top of Tumalo Falls. Still further, you can follow the creek along the trail and suddenly you will be engulfed in a forest of fir, hemlock, manzanita, and other native vegetation. If you like to camp, Happy Valley awaits or you can make a loop and return to the parking lot. In my opinion, the greatest rewards are those buried deeper in the forest.

541-383-4000
fs.usda.gov

HIKE MISERY RIDGE TRAIL
AND LIVE TO TELL ABOUT IT
AT SMITH ROCK

Central Oregon is full of natural wonders and picturesque landscapes. Smith Rock State Park in Terrebonne is up near the top of that list. Although you will never catch me scaling the massive rhyolite rock formations, the park is a paradise among the rock-climbing community. For those of us content enjoying the scenery with two feet on the ground, hiking is a fulfilling alternative. Misery Ridge Trail, the most popular, meanders through deep canyons and climbs up and down steep ridges to give awesome views of the Crooked River and the Cascade snow peaks. The hike is not easy, but the incomparable views make every step worth the effort. Try to spot golden eagles soaring high, magpies in the brush, or other wildlife following their daily routine. Most likely you will see climbers along the route and stare up at them in awe, especially if they are dangling from the towering Monkey Face Rock, the park's most iconic feature. I have the utmost respect for those brave souls!

Smith Rock State Park, Terrebonne, 541-516-0054
smithrock.com

TIP

On any trail, always take plenty of water, snacks, and sunscreen. And please follow basic hiking etiquette, which is usually posted in several areas. Stay on the trails. Keep dogs on a leash. Don't create new parking spaces. These rules are in place for a reason, to keep these scenic areas protected and beautiful. Don't be that guy (or girl) who says to themselves, "Well, if I do it, it's OK." If everyone thought that way, these areas would lose a lot of what makes them so special.

EXPLORE UNDERGROUND
INSIDE THE LAVA RIVER CAVE

Can you imagine a river of molten lava from an erupting volcano flowing underground and carving a tunnel? Can you believe that nowadays you can actually walk through the same spot? At the Newberry National Monument, you can descend into darkness of the Lava River Cave and witness what the dynamic forces of nature have created over thousands of years. You'll be fascinated by lavacicles, gardens of spires and pinnacles in the sand, and other unique cave features. You may hear a stranger's conversations in Echo Hall. If you really fancy yourself a spelunker, you can explore the last few hundred feet of the cave on your hands and knees. The cave is open from May through September. Bring a flashlight and be sure to wear a jacket. It gets chilly down there!

Newberry National Monument
541-383-4000
fs.usda.gov

TRAIL RUN
THROUGH ARCHIE BRIGGS CANYON

Miles and miles of amazing trails. Which is the best for running? I'd say try to run all of them eventually, but a favorite of mine is through the Archie Briggs Canyon. Part of the Deschutes River Trail, you will forget about distance and complexity and instead let the spectacular surroundings guide your way. From high cliffs, gaze down at the roaring river. Dash through manzanita, rabbitbrush, and sagebrush. During summer, wildflowers like the Indian Paintbrush will brighten your run with colors. Depending on how far you want to go, you can start or stop at several points, the farther the better. A good nature run is not only good for your physical health, but for your mental and spiritual health as well. What are you waiting for? Get outside!

hikespeak.com/trails/archie-briggs-canyon-hike-bend-oregon

PRETEND TO EXPLORE ANOTHER PLANET
AT NEWBERRY NATIONAL MONUMENT

About 1,300 years ago, the Newberry Volcano erupted in Central Oregon. Though still a hot spot (pun intended) of volcanic activity, the threat of a possible eruption doesn't stop people from moving here in droves. At Newberry National Monument you can witness thousands of years' worth of geologic upheaval that created this magnificent landscape. As you walk trails like the Big Obsidian Flow, you'll notice jagged obsidian gleaming brightly in the sun. These shiny black rocks combined with the pumice and lack of vegetation make you feel as if you are walking on another planet. In fact, astronauts trained here in the 1960s! From the Paulina Peak Trail you get a panorama of Central Oregon and the Newberry Caldera. There are so many trails to explore, and each gives different aspects of these otherworldly geologic features. Stop by the Lava Lands Visitor Center to get more information.

Lava Lands Visitor Center
58201 US-97, 541-383-5300
fs.usda.gov

FEED THE CUTE ALPACAS
AT CRESCENT MOON RANCH

Driving along Highway 97, you stare out of the window and suddenly notice a bunch of cute, furry creatures in the fields. "Were those alpacas?" your child asks as the family does a double take. Alpacas are not something you see every day, but if you drive by Crescent Moon Ranch, there they are, waiting for a visit. Stop by and interact with them while the ranch is open. You can purchase a small bag of grain, feed them, all the while taking in the picturesque views of Smith Rock and the Cascade Mountains in the background. An on-site boutique sells items made from the highly sought-after alpaca fiber, known to be some of the most luxurious in the world. After getting to know some of their distinct personalities, you may even want to take an alpaca home. And guess what? You can! Just ask the owners for details before loading one up in the car.

7566 N Hwy. 97, Terrebonne, 541-923-2285
crescentmoonranch.com

LEARN A NEW SKILL OR IMPROVE AN EXISTING ONE
WITH BEND PARKS & RECREATION

Bend Parks & Recreation runs such a well-developed, well-orchestrated citywide organization that other cities should take notes. Besides keeping the numerous parks around town immaculately clean and landscaped, they offer so many opportunities to the community. Camps, free play days, after-school programs, recreational activities, tours, and year-round classes are available for every age group. Want to take martial arts? Learn how to snow ski? Build a robot? Paint? Take a trip abroad? Whatever your interest, you will almost certainly find an activity to guide you in the right direction. Bend is a tight-knit community, and Bend Parks & Recreation is the glue that keeps it together and thriving.

541-389-7275
bendparksandrec.org/activities

GET FIT OR TAKE A DIP
AT JUNIPER FITNESS & SWIM

In a city where outdoor sports reign supreme, health is a top priority. Run by Bend Parks & Recreation, Juniper Fitness & Swim is my go-to place when I can't get outside. More than an average gym, the clean facilities, modern equipment, outdoor and indoor pools, saunas, and much more create the perfect environment for health and wellness. Juniper has countless family activities and classes available, ranging from yoga to cycling to swimming and more. Not a member? No worries, they have flexible options to meet your needs. Purchase a punch card that allows several visits at your convenience with access to all the amenities. Drop-ins are welcome as well. If you want to stay fit and healthy and be part of a tight-knit community, this is your place. A newer facility, Larkspur Community Center, is now open as well.

Juniper Fitness & Swim
800 NE 6th St., 541-389-7665
bendparksandrec.org/fitness-swim/juniper-swim-fitness

Larkspur Community Center
1600 SE Reed Market Rd., 541-388-1133
bendparksandrec.org/facility/larkspur-community-center

STEP
ON A CRACK-IN-THE-GROUND

You might ask, "What's so great about a Crack-in-the-Ground? I can look down at the sidewalk to see one of those." Well, you can hike at the bottom of this one. Around 70 feet deep and two miles long, the crack is really a large volcanic fissure. Since the climate of Christmas Valley is so dry, it has never been filled up with soil and rock, meaning it hasn't changed much in thousands of years. But as dry as the area is, you will be pleasantly surprised. On scorching hot days, a hike through the crack can actually be refreshing. The temperature is 20 degrees cooler at the bottom. Bright green moss stretches up the cliffs where birds fly to and from their nests. And if you want a quieter hike, often free from the crowds, you've come to the right place.

Christmas Valley, OR
blm.gov/visit/crack-ground

TIP

When making the drive through Christmas Valley to Crack-in-the-Ground, check out Fort Rock as well. The large, half-moon shaped tuff ring that is now recognized as a state park was once completely underwater. Believe it or not, this dry, flat area used to be part of an inland ocean. In Fort Rock Cave, sandals made from bark and sagebrush dating around 10,000 years old were found! You may not find any more of those, but it's still pretty awesome to explore where some of our ancestors roamed so long ago.

REACH NEW HEIGHTS
AT BEND ROCK GYM

For those not quite ready to climb real rock formations like those mentioned at Smith Rock State Park, the Bend Rock Gym still promises a sense of adventure. It also offers serious climbers the chance to hone their skills when they might not have time to get to the real rocks. Three types of admission allow you to climb on your own schedule: day passes, punch cards, and monthly memberships. Bring your own or rent gear and climb until you are sore. Oh yeah, you will feel it the next day. All levels are welcome, even young children. Most employees are experienced climbers who can guide and give safety tips. Talk about a great way to test your toughness and develop a skill! The higher you go the higher your adrenaline and confidence gets.

1182 SE Centennial Ct., 541-388-6764
bendrockgym.com

BREATHE IN THE SWEET SMELLS
OF TUMALO LAVENDER

At Tumalo Lavender the breeze carries a delightful aroma through the air; go there and immediately you will feel relaxed and calm. Shades of purple stretch across the 10-acre farm and represent the many varieties of the meticulously planted rows of lavender. The pinkish-purple plant grows exceptionally well in the Pacific Northwest, and this place proves it. Walk through the fields and admire the countless butterflies and bees playfully pollinating the plants. Gordon and Judy Knight, the owners, will happily explain anything you want to know about lavender and show you the elaborate process by which they make the oil. Meanwhile, their friendly dog chills out lazily in the fields. After a short while at the farm, the scents will most likely have you so relaxed you may be ready for a nap!

19825 Connarn Rd., 541-383-2441
tumalolavender.com

STAND ON TOP OF A VOLCANO
AT PILOT BUTTE STATE PARK

Yes, you read the intro correctly. Bend is one of the few cities in the United States to have a volcano located within the city limits. No worries though, Pilot Butte isn't erupting anytime soon—at least we hope not! For the best experience, start an hour or so before sunset and hike one of the mile-long trails to the summit. Along the trails, the strong scent of juniper trees and other high desert brush quickly makes you forget you are still in the city. If you prefer an easier route, drive the scenic road that lazily spirals around the cone. It's open most of the year but closes during winter. On top, breathe the crisp air and peer out at the amazing 360-degree view of the entire city, the high desert, and the magnificent Cascade Mountains. Then try to fathom the fact that you are standing on top of a volcano!

541-388-6949
oregonstateparks.org

FUN FACT

Remember I mentioned other cities with
volcanos inside the city limits? The others are:

Mount Tabor in Portland, Oregon

Diamond Head in Honolulu, Hawaii

Mount Jackson in Jackson, Mississippi
(Who would have guessed Mississippi?!)

HELP GROW A GARDEN
AT THE ENVIRONMENTAL CENTER

Calling all eager volunteers! During the summer months, children (and adults) are invited to help grow a garden at the Environmental Center. In this outdoor classroom, volunteers get their hands dirty by planting tomatoes, peppers, and other veggies, and caring for them during growing season. One minute they might be digging or making observations and the next minute they might be chasing another kid around the garden. What better way to learn about where our food comes from? The adults often help, and for their effort are generously furnished tasty beverages. Hey, anyone working in the garden (especially with kids) deserves a drink! The Environmental Center also offers lots of other year-round community activities and educational events that share the importance of sustainable and regenerative gardening. Be sure to check those out as well.

16 NW Kansas Ave., 541-385-6908
envirocenter.org

EXPERIENCE THE TRUE OREGON DESERT
IN THE BADLANDS

Often, people have a misinformed stereotype of Oregon. They picture gray skies and endless rain. Little do they realize that roughly a quarter of the state is desert with little precipitation. Enter the Badlands Wilderness. A true taste of the high desert, this vast area expands almost 30,000 acres. Sandy trails lead through ancient rock formations, gnarly looking juniper trees, sagebrush, rabbitbrush, and native grasses. Beautiful in its own right, this once chaotic region now provides a quiet, peaceful experience, with the occasional sounds of the blowing wind or the chirping of birds. And, when other trails are still packed with snow or ice, those here are the first to be clear and easily walkable. This is a place where much violent volcanic activity took place in the past, and you can witness it in the remarkable geological features of the landscape.

Oregon Badlands Wilderness
blm.gov/visit/oregon-badlands-wilderness

TIP

For the most adventurous among us, the Oregon Badlands are also the western gateway to the Oregon Desert Trail, an almost 750-mile trail that leads through Steens Mountain, Lake Owyhee State Park, Hart Mountain National Antelope Range, and numerous other fascinating landscapes in Oregon. Are you ready to become a thru-hiker?

CULTURE
AND HISTORY

BECOME AN ART CRITIC
ON THE FIRST FRIDAY ART WALK

Every first Friday of the month, lively crowds descend on the streets of downtown Bend and the Old Mill District to enjoy the First Friday Art Walk. The event has become a popular tradition in the city, and, yes, you will see paintings and sculptures and such, but during the night you will also be able to appreciate the many other types of artists displaying their skills. Think about the chef who cooks the food, the musician, the clothing designer, the vintner, the photographer, the jewelry maker: all are artists of their craft. Dozens of businesses stay open late, many offering live music and free snacks and drinks. The night is an amazing opportunity to mingle with friends, meet new people, and celebrate the city's eclectic and diverse art scene.

Downtown & Old Mill District
bendfirstfridayartwalk.com

SOAK UP THE HISTORY OF CENTRAL OREGON
AT DESCHUTES HISTORICAL MUSEUM

Once upon a time, the Deschutes Historical Museum housed rowdy yet studious schoolchildren in what was the first "modern school" built in Bend. Nowadays, it houses an in-depth view into the history of Central Oregon. Browse the building to get educated. Ms. Reid's schoolroom travels back in time to what a classroom looked like over 100 years ago. My kids wanted to spend most of the visit playing teacher and student in this room. Logging, which has shaped Oregon's past tremendously, is detailed in the Forests of Oregon. Still other rooms have artifacts and information about Native Americans, homesteading, and the earliest days of Bend. If you have questions after visiting the rooms, be sure to ask the staff. They are an encyclopedia of information when it comes to the intriguing history of the area.

129 NW Idaho Ave., 541-389-1813
deschuteshistory.org

EXPLORE THE CLIMATE OF CENTRAL OREGON
AT THE HIGH DESERT MUSEUM

Oregon gets a bad rap for being wet and dreary much of the year. Not so in this part of the state. The high desert enjoys sunshine most of the year. At the High Desert Museum, the story of Central Oregon's climate is told through art, Native American history, science, wildlife, and more. All these mediums create a textured and interactive learning experience that makes both kids and adults want to return again and again. With 9–12 rotating exhibits, you can never get enough. Permanent exhibits like the Spirit of the West display the history of the Paiute people and other past residents of Central Oregon. Residents like the otters and the porcupines are local favorites. My family is partial to the mighty raptors at the Birds of Prey Center. There is nothing quite like witnessing the power or looking into the eyes of a bald eagle up close.

59800 US-97, 541-382-4754
highdesertmuseum.org

LOITER IN THE ALLEYS
OF DOWNTOWN BEND

The Tin Pan Alley Art Collection livens up the alleys, the parking garages, and other parts of downtown Bend. With more than a dozen pieces and growing, the city has transformed these usually dingy, smelly areas into culturally significant attractions. Blink an eye and you might not find it, but Tin Pan Alley itself is absolutely worth a stop. Take a self-guided tour to view paintings like *The Visitor* or *Love Lost, Love Found* that hang patiently on the brick buildings. While there, catch an independent film at Tin Pan Theater, an almost hidden microcinema with an intimate retro vibe. Enjoy a drink and "sophisticated debauchery" at San Simón. Never in a city have you seen alleyways so inviting! An extension of the public art can be found at the Old Mill District as well.

Tin Pan Alley Art Collection
visitbend.com/things-to-do/art-museums-history/arts/tin-pan-alley-art

Tin Pan Theater
867 NW Tin Pan Alley, 541-241-2271
tinpantheater.com

San Simón
845 Tin Pan Alley, 541-323-0235
sansimonbend.com

ADMIRE UNIQUE ART
WHILE DRIVING THE ROUNDABOUTS

When driving in Bend, you may get the feeling you are in Europe with all the roundabouts! They take some getting used to, but you will quickly notice that many roundabouts in Bend have stunning works of art in the middle. In fact, soon you will be driving out of your way to make sure you find *Phoenix Rising*, *Soundgarden* (not the band), and *Sunrise Spirit Column* (a few of my favorites). I would not advise stopping in busy traffic to take a pic or admire the art, but there are usually places to park nearby. Bend has over 20 sculptures in total and searching for them all is a great way to get to know the city. *Yakaya* is my overall favorite, a large flower-like sculpture made from real, colorful kayaks and located in River Bend Park. Pretty impressive!

All around town
artinpublicplaces.org/roundabout.html

TIP

Visit Bend has a Roundabout Art Route
brochure with a map and detailed information
about each of the art installations. And, like the
Bend Ale Trail, you can visit several of them,
return to the visitor's center, and claim a prize!
Be sure to pay attention to what you see,
though, because they quiz you on this one!

SPEND A DAY (OR MORE)
IN SISTERS

Most states tend to have that one little town full of culture and vibrant energy, an area that seems to draw artists to it. In Oregon, that town is arguably Sisters, located about half an hour from Bend. With the glorious backdrop of mountains, the town itself could be a painting. On a visit, begin the morning by grabbing a coffee from Sisters Coffee so you have something to sip as you leisurely walk the lively streets. Stop at local shops like Paulina Springs Books and The Stitchin' Post. Visit as many galleries as possible along the way and view the public art as well. You will be amazed by the talent and variety of what you see and perhaps be inspired to create your own art, or at least leave Sisters with new items to decorate your home.

Sisters
sistersoregonguide.com

Paulina Springs Books
252 W Hood Ave., 541-549-0866
paulinaspringsbooks.com

The Stitchin' Post
311 W Cascade St., 541-549-6061
stitchinpost.com

Sisters Coffee
273 W Hood Ave., 541-549-0527
sisterscoffee.com

FEEL THE HEART OF BEND
IN THE OLD MILL DISTRICT

Before it became the booming tourist town of today, Bend was home to two of the largest lumber mills in the country. World War I produced a large demand for timber, and by the end of World War II the beautiful forests of the West were nearly decimated. Fast forward to the present. Standing in the middle of the Old Mill District you are in an outdoor, modern-day shopping mall, but this spot is exactly where the mills were located, and the rivers were jammed with logs. Walk along the trail adjacent to Deschutes River and among the shops and restaurants to read the interpretive signs about Bend's past as a mill town. To see the pictures of what the area used to look like compared to the present is really phenomenal, proof that we can sustain and even regenerate an area. The biggest tribute to the city's past is the large iconic smokestacks towering above the REI building, which can be seen from almost anywhere in Bend. Elsewhere, the concrete foundation for a mill powerhouse remains anachronistically intact and hosts colorful flowers in spring. Modern murals, paintings (part of the Tin Pan Alley Art Collection), and sculptures are also strewn throughout the district, creating the perfect mixture of Bend's proud past and present. The city is working hard to ensure its future as well.

450 SW Powerhouse Dr., #422, 541-312-0131
oldmilldistrict.com

WALK THE HISTORIC SITES
OF BEND

Incorporated in 1904, Bend is relatively young compared to many cities, but it still has a deep history. Like many cities around the world, it built up around a river. If you feel like getting educated about the past, pick up a free Bend Historic Sites map at the Deschutes Historical Museum. The building is also #1 on the list. From there, all 45 locations on the map are located within walking distance. You can take a leisurely stroll and visit places like Alexander Drake's homesite (the founder of Bend) and the J. J. West Building (the town's first stone structure). Some locations have plaques with detailed information. The walk is definitely doable in a day, but you can also break it up and take as long as you like. By the time you finish you will be a Central Oregon history expert!

Bend Historic Sites
All around town

Deschutes Historical Museum
129 NW Idaho Ave., 541-389-1813
deschuteshistory.org

TIP

The DHM launched a phone app to
help find points of interest in the area. The
"Cruisin' 97" feature gives a list and locations
of historic landmarks around Highway 97.
Each entry has a photo, a bit of history,
and links to read further information.
Download it by searching "Deschutes
Historical Museum" in any app store.

PONDER THE COSMOS WHILE YOU DRINK A BREW
AT WORTHY HOPSERVATORY

Space, the final frontier. You're philosophizing with friends over drinks about our place in the vast universe. The sky is clear with a new moon and the stars are shining brightly. You decide to get up from the patio and walk upstairs to the Hopservatory to view the cosmos more closely. Located at Worthy Brewing (yes, the brewery), begin your tour of the Hopservatory downstairs in the Transporter Room, where the walls and a large, 12-foot pier are cosmically decorated with mosaic tiles that illustrate the universe. TV monitors provide information. Walk upstairs to the Dome and get a stunning panorama from Mount Hood to Mount Bachelor. On Thursday through Sunday evenings and sometimes during special "lunar" events, Grant Tandy, the Hopservatory's resident astronomer, will show you the brightest objects in the sky through the powerful telescope. Combining astronomy and a night out with friends has never been so fun!

495 NE Bellevue Dr., 541-639-4776
worthygardenclub.com/hopservatory

VIEW GALAXIES FAR FAR AWAY
AT PINE MOUNTAIN OBSERVATORY

There are billions and billions of stars in the sky, and with the bright city lights we can barely see them. Not so in this part of Oregon. In the less-populated parts of Central Oregon, the stars are fascinating even with the naked eye. But to really be awestruck, a visit to the Pine Mountain Observatory is mandatory. The mixture of elevation, clean air, and pitch-dark surroundings allow for perfect stargazing conditions. Although the observatory is used mostly for research, on weekends from Memorial Day until the end of September anyone can visit and get intimate with the cosmos. Astronomers on hand will point out the visible features of the night sky to the novice. On a clear evening you will leave mesmerized and in deep thought about our place in the universe.

57245 River Rd., Sunriver, 541-589-4406
pmo.uoregon.edu

WITNESS AWESOMENESS
WHEN VIEWING THE MURALS OF BEND

Perhaps you see a giant octopus on the wall while driving down Third Street or the silhouette of cowboys while driving the speed limit on Highway 97. Maybe the colorful, graffiti-style dragon in the Old Mill catches your eye when floating the Deschutes. These and many other imaginative murals are scattered all around Bend. Lucky for us, the city has encouraged artists to liven up our public spaces with their creative visions. Some murals are playful and entertaining like Erik Hoogan's *Mixtape* at Silver Moon Brewing. Featuring musical artists ranging from Eazy-E to Dolly Parton, the time and skill it took to create these intricate, lifelike depictions is amazing, and it's always fun to discover a new face. Other paintings have deeper meanings or tell a story like *Born Again Babaylan* by Bekah Badilla located on a wall of MacTek. These visionary expressions add flavor and richness to our city, and I hope they continue to fill our public spaces.

All around Bend

TIP

For an entertaining way to see many of the murals, check out the Ultimate Scavenger Bend: Murals, a scavenger hunt that takes you around town and gives a bit of background about each of these amazing works of art.

bendmarketplace.com/?s=murals

RAISE YOUR AWARENESS
AT SUNRIVER NATURE CENTER

Even wild animals like ospreys, eagles, and beavers need a little love and affection. Often, they are sick or hurt and need to be rescued. Fortunately, places like Sunriver Nature Center exist as a sanctuary for birds and small mammals. And while the center attempts to rehabilitate them, we get to learn. Knowledgeable experts teach all about the birds of prey and other local native species. Visitors can get up close and personal with amphibians or snakes. Strolls through the botanical garden and around the Aspen Lake Loop give glimpses of native plants and maybe an occasional otter. When you find yourself wanting to know more about local wildlife, or maybe you've made friends with a resident raptor, the center is a perfect day trip.

57245 River Rd., Sunriver, 541-593-4442
sunrivernaturecenter.org

TIP

Adjacent to the Sunriver Nature Center sits the Oregon Observatory. When the sun sets, the largest collection of public telescopes in the entire US is available for us to look through at the beauty and brilliance of the night sky!

BECOME MESMERIZED BY THE ART
OF ALFRED A. DOLEZAL

Visionary artist Alfred A. Dolezal is originally from Austria, but he has lived in Central Oregon for many years. A trip to his gallery in Redmond is one you will remember. In his paintings, the vivid colors seem to jump out of the canvas. The profound symbolism may take a lifetime to uncover and gets your mind thinking deeply. Works such as *Triumph Over Adversity* and *The Harmony of Opposites* are based on timeless parables. *The Light Through the Ages* depicts the many people who have influenced not only Alfred, but all of human progress. Behind every painting is an intricate story. If you are lucky, the artist himself may be at the gallery to explain his thought process while he created each work. Prepare to question your own beliefs and become mesmerized by an amazingly talented artist.

7525 Falcon Crest Dr., Ste. 100, Redmond, 541-526-1185
alfreddolezal.com

SHOPPING
AND FASHION

SHOP TILL YOU DROP
AT THE OLD MILL DISTRICT

In the heart of the city also rests Bend's biggest shopping area, the Old Mill District. With over 40 stores, several restaurants, and a movie theater, this open-air mall is nestled on the Deschutes River. You will find many of the well-known anchor stores like Victoria's Secret, Claire's, REI, Banana Republic, and other favorites as well as local shops. Restaurants for all tastes are scattered about. It's not a bad place to just hang out either. For those waiting on the shoppers in their group, take a walk on the bridge or the paved trails to enjoy beautiful views of the river and mountains. Browse the art scattered throughout the area. You can even bring your running shoes and get some exercise while everyone else in your group spends money!

450 SW Powerhouse Dr., #422, 541-312-0131
oldmilldistrict.com

STAY FASHIONABLE
AT REVOLVR AND
VANILLA URBAN THREADS

Searching for the latest men's or women's fashions? For men, REVOLVR is a local favorite for the most stylish apparel and accessories in Bend. Rarely do I leave the store without purchasing something fresh to wear. And do not be surprised if the staff offer you a beer taster when you walk in, an added bonus. Many ladies claim Vanilla Urban Threads as a favorite for women's clothing. They love it, and when you walk inside it's easy to see why. The impressive variety of unique and stylish apparel, swimsuits, hats, shoes, jewelry, candles, and other gifts make Vanilla Urban a one-stop shop. They have stuff for guys as well. No matter what season, these locations should be the first choice when buying some new threads. You'll feel like a new person when you walk out the door.

REVOLVR Menswear
945 NW Wall St., 541-647-2627
revolvrmens.com

Vanilla Urban Threads
661 SW Powerhouse Dr., #1302, 541-617-6113
shopvanilla.com

EXPAND YOUR CHILD'S IMAGINATION
AT LEAPIN' LIZARDS

Perhaps you recognize the phrase "Leapin' Lizards" from the original *Annie* movie (by the way, the remake is pretty good as well). Say the phrase in Bend and the first thing that comes to mind is the Leapin' Lizards Toy Company. This downtown fun spot has been fulfilling kids' wish lists since 1995! Still going strong, the colorful shop doesn't carry just any toys found on the shelves of the big box stores. Sure, they have Legos, water guns, action figures, and the like, but when is the last time you saw a Lite Brite or the classic game Operation? They carefully handpick items that encourage kids to be creative and use their imagination. Focused on stimulating an environment of play and growth, the store has chemistry sets, art easels, activity books, puzzles, and other fun stuff. Youthful adults can find something for themselves as well. Sometimes, we all need to unleash the kid inside of us and this is the place to do it!

953 NW Wall St.
leapinlizardstoys.com

SUPPORT LOCAL BUSINESSES
ON THE BEND MARKETPLACE

The Bend Marketplace is an online, one-stop shop for almost everything offered in Bend. Created to support local businesses during the tougher time of the pandemic shutdowns, the website has grown rapidly to include every imaginable product and service. Art, clothing, soap, candles, massages, restaurants, gift certificates, language lessons, tech, tickets for concerts and other live events, adventure activities—you name it, the Bend Marketplace likely has it! The *Source Weekly*, the city's weekly newspaper, paired up with the market and features "Source Perks," coupons for favorite shops and services. Bend is a hot spot full of entrepreneurial creatives, and the Bend Marketplace brings the community to you. After shopping online at the site, you may never leave the house again. Support local!

Bend Marketplace
bendmarketplace.com

EXPAND YOUR IMAGINATION
AT A LOCAL BOOKSTORE

I can spend hours in a bookstore. Hours pass by without a care in the world. Bend boasts some exceptional bookstores, each distinctive in its own way. Dudley's Bookshop Cafe has a great location downtown. The selection of new and used books coupled with tasty beverages and snacks make it a local favorite. Nearby, Pegasus Books boasts a unique selection of new books, and its collection of graphic novels, manga, comics, and other collectables is second to none. Big Story, recently beautified with the colorful owl mural that can be seen from Third Street, has a thoughtfully curated selection, both used and new. Nearby, Bend Coffee & Books is a quiet used bookstore and a great spot to escape to and enjoy a drink or food item. The neighborhood feel of Roundabout Books in Northwest Crossing makes one feel at home instantly. They also host regular author talks and signings. Whether you're an avid reader, need a tranquil spot to relax, or are looking for a birthday present, these shops are a gift to us all. Bounce around and support each of them.

Dudley's Bookshop Cafe
13 NW Minnesota Ave., 541-749-2010
dudleysbookshopcafe.com

Roundabout Books
900 NW Mount Washington, Ste. 110, 541-306-6564
roundaboutbookshop.com

Big Story
228 NE Greenwood Ave., 541-617-9271
bigstorybend.com

Pegasus Books
105 NW Minnesota Ave., 541-388-4588
pegasusbooksofbend.blogspot.com

Bend Coffee & Books
155 NE Greenwood Ave., 541-388-3249

PICK UP A SOUVENIR
AT THE BEND STORE/CASCADE COTTONS

Two places come to mind when I'm buying something for friends and family (or myself) with the famous Bend logo. Yep, the city has its own logo and even its own font. How many cities can say that? For clothing, especially T-shirts, Cascade Cottons has a large selection of awesome designs, many of which sport the Bend trademark. Nearby and more than a typical souvenir shop, the Bend Store has the types of items you might expect to find: coffee mugs, stickers, magnets, ornaments, and more. However, as a hub for local artists, you will also discover handcrafted jewelry, art, and other unique treasures at the shop. Bendites are proud of their city and for good reason. Don't leave without a quality souvenir to remind you of the good times you spent in Central Oregon.

Cascade Cottons
909 NW Wall St., 541-306-6071
cascadecottons.com

The Bend Store
815 NW Wall St., 541-389-4700
bendstore.com

BUILD YOUR VINYL COLLECTION
AT SMITH ROCK RECORDS

Vinyl just sounds better, and no doubt it has been making a comeback. Every city (or at least every hip city) should have a record store. Smith Rock Records boasts Bend's largest collection of vinyl, CDs, concert videos, and even some cassette tapes. But don't think it's all older music. Some of us forget that new artists still put their music out on vinyl and CDs. The shop also has the best collection of concert posters I've ever seen and from all genres: Snoop Dogg, Widespread Panic, Pearl Jam, The Beatles, and more. Of course, as they sell, new ones take their place. Many of the posters are even autographed. Back in the '90s I used to get super hyped for Tuesdays when new music was released at the local music shop. Nowadays, it's new music Fridays, but any time I walk into Smith Rock Records I get excited about music again!

117 NW Oregon Ave., 541-389-6116
facebook.com/smithrockrecords

PREP WITH OUTDOOR GEAR
FROM PINE MOUNTAIN SPORTS & POWDER HOUSE

What if you are visiting the area to play outside and don't have any gear? Or just want to try a new outdoor sport to see if you like it before spending a fortune? Local shops in Bend are here to solve this predicament, and two are especially helpful. From snowboards and snowshoes to Nordic skis and everything in between, Powder House has the largest inventory of winter gear in the area. Add reasonable prices and a helpful staff and it is easy to see why it was voted "Bend's Best Ski & Snowboard Shop." Pine Mountain Sports has more mountain bikes than you can imagine. No worries for the novice, because they will help you choose the right bike for the right ride. They also rent winter gear. When I moved to Central Oregon, I had never snow skied, nor did I know exactly which bike would be best for different types of terrain. Luckily, these two shops exist to share their expertise.

Pine Mountain Sports
255 SW Century Dr., 541-385-8080
pinemountainsports.com

Powder House
311 SW Century Dr., 541-389-6234
powderhousebend.com

GET YOUR OUTDOOR GEAR
AT GEAR FIX

If you've read this far in the book, you realize that Bend is the ultimate hub for adventure, full of people who respect and love the outdoors. Unfortunately, outdoor gear can get pricey, and smart shoppers want to purchase the best equipment at the best price. Time for a visit to Gear Fix! Located in the Box Factory, the store buys, sells, and trades most anything an outdoor enthusiast can imagine. Biking, skiing, hiking, climbing; if it's something used for an outside activity, chances are they have it. Planning to get rid of your old gear? The store will try to sell your items on consignment. And not only does Gear Fix sell clothing and equipment, they also can repair almost anything, from the soles of your shoes to the helmet on your head!

550 SW Industrial Way, #183, 541-617-0022
gearfix.com

LOAD UP ON ANTIQUES AND COLLECTABLES
IN REDMOND

Antique hunters, I haven't forgotten about you. Decades of elusive treasures await in Redmond. Beyond the Ranch, the Farmer's Co-op, and the Redmond Antique Mall are huge and contain an amazing accumulation of everything imaginable. I'm not talking about junk here, I'm talking about high-quality and often historic and valuable items: furniture, books, china, coins, tools, toys, jewelry, military and farm equipment, typewriters, old phone booths—I could go on forever! Every nook and cranny in these shops is filled with something interesting. Going with my young daughters and explaining the uses of things from the past is an education in itself. "What do you mean phones used to have a cord?" You can also find Central Oregon's best collection of comics and collectables at Geek Geek Nerd Nerd, the comic shop located next door to the Redmond Antique Mall building. Make an adventurous day of it!

The Redmond Farmer's Co-op Antique Mall
106 SE Evergreen Ave., #A, 541-548-7975
facebook.com/redmondfarmerscoop

Redmond Antique Mall
106 SE Evergreen Ave., Ste. M, 541-548-6208
redmondantiquemall.com

Beyond the Ranch Antiques
339 SW Evergreen Ave., 541-279-4867
beyond-the-ranch.com

Geek Geek Nerd Nerd
106 SE Evergreen Ave., Ste. J, 541-527-4987
facebook.com/geekgeeknerdnerd

FILL YOUR FRIDGE WITH CULINARY DELIGHTS
FROM NEWPORT AVENUE MARKET

When it's time to fill the fridge with the finest foods, Newport Avenue Market should be the first thought that comes to mind. An employee-owned business, the market has the area's best selection of cheeses, meats, seafood, olive oils, and other specialty food items. Aisles of locally inspired gifts, cookware, books, and other novelty items also await. The Spirit Shop and endless choices of fine wines ensure that those enthusiasts are not to be forgotten, while the "Great Wall of Beer" has over 600 beers, most likely the largest collection in Bend! The helpful staff prides themselves on helping with recommendations for recipes and such. Outside the market, snap a pic of the colorful *Bend Wall* mural by Kim Smallenberg. Hang out in the shaded patio area with Bigfoot while enjoying something delicious from the bakery or deli. Before you go, be sure to give the bear a big hug.

1121 NW Newport Ave., 541-382-3940
newportavemarket.com

ACTIVITIES
BY SEASON

SPRING

SUMMER

· ·

FALL

WINTER

SUGGESTED
ITINERARIES

AN EVENING DOWNTOWN WITH ADULTS

Become an Art Critic on the First Friday Art Walk, 100

Fine Dine from A–Z in Bend, 21

Catch a Performance at Tower Theatre, 38

Relish Some Grown-Up Time at Velvet, 4

A DAY WITH KIDS

Stroll through Drake Park, 79

Imagine a Trip to Italy at Bonta, 12

Satisfy Your Sweet Tooth at Cravin's, 7

Explore the Climate of Central Oregon
  at the High Desert Museum, 102

Expand Your Child's Imagination at Leapin' Lizards, 120

A SHORT STAY IN BEND

Bond with Nature on the Deschutes River Trail, 62

Float or Paddleboard the Deschutes River, 73

Stand on Top of a Volcano at Pilot Butte State Park, 94

Do Your Best Jack Nicholson Impression at Worthy Brewing, 10

Pick Up a Souvenir at the Bend Store/Cascade Cottons, 124

Absorb the Sunset at Crux Fermentation, 19

• •

FREE STUFF

EXTREME FUN IN CENTRAL OREGON

GETTING STARTED ON THE BEND ALE TRAIL

OUTDOORS WITH THE KIDS

• •

INDEX

● ●

● ●

• •

● ●